Intermittent Fasting
A Beginner's Guidebook for Men and Women to Challenge Crash Diets and Achieve Effective Weight Loss and Fitness Naturally

By: Emily Simmons

While every precaution has been taken in the preparation of this book, the publisher assumes no responsibility for errors or omissions, or for damages resulting from the use of the information contained herein.

INTERMITTENT FASTING

First edition. November 25, 2018.

Copyright © 2018 Emily Simmons.

ISBN: 978-1386978206

Written by Emily Simmons.

Introduction: A Brief Prelude to Intermittent Fasting

Chapter One: How Does Intermittent Fasting Work and What Are Its Benefits

Chapter Two: Some Myths Busted and Who Should Avoid Intermittent Fasting

Chapter Three: Methods of Intermittent Fasting

Chapter Four: Tips to Start off, What to Expect in the Initial Days and How to Manage Them

Chapter Five: Intermittent Fasting and Weight Loss

Chapter Six: Mistakes to Avoid and Other Important Information about Intermittent Fasting

Conclusion

Introduction: A Brief Prelude to Intermittent Fasting

Intermittent fasting is not a diet but merely an eating pattern. Fasting is one of the most natural forms of healing that has been in existence from time immemorial. It is not just humans but even animals that do not eat when they are sick. Resting the digestive system during times of physical stress such as an illness facilitates improved healing naturally.

You don't need to go very far to understand the connection between fasting to illness. Recall the last time you fell sick. It could be something as simple as a cold-cough or a bout of viral flu. During that time, the thought of food brought on a feeling of nausea, right? That was a sign from your body urging you to abstain from eating until your sickness was healed.

Any living being's natural instinct is to stay away from food during sickness to allow the body to begin the healing process. When the healing is completed, the appetite will return naturally. The ancient Greek physician, Hippocrates, said, *"To eat when you are sick is like feeding the sickness."* Plutarch, another philosopher and wise man from the ancient Greek-Roman times, said, *"Instead of using medicine, rather, fast a day."*

So, what is intermittent fasting? Here is a brief answer to this question. The modern world calls for eating 3-4 (sometimes 4-6 small meals too) meals a day including breakfast, lunch, a small snack with your afternoon tea and dinner. Intermittent fasting calls for reducing the number of meals from 3-4 to 1-2. Other than this, there are few restrictions on what you can eat. Before we go into the details of intermittent fasting, how it works, its various benefits, and how to implement it in your life, let us delve into its history briefly.

History of Intermittent Fasting

In the prehistoric times, our hunter-gatherer ancestors had no option but to fast because they had food only when they achieved a good hunting session. On days when their hunt was unsuccessful, they would starve or simply eat what little berries or fruits they could gather. Unwittingly or otherwise, they reaped the benefits of fasting. They were muscular, sturdy and healthy and survived through some of the most difficult times in human history, battling wild animals, extreme climates, harsh living conditions etc.

The ancient civilizations including the Greeks, the Sumerians, the people of the Indus Valley Civilizations, the Egyptians, and others used fasting as a method of healing the body. Records that prove the use of 'starvation' to help in the recovery of a diseased or sick body and even as a preventive measure have been unearthed in many places. These ancient and wise civilizations were keenly aware of and employed the benefits of fasting and intermittent fasting to improve their health.

In many religions, fasting was used to reflect self-control and/or as a form of penitence. Let us look at some of the world religions and their deep connection to fasting:

Judaism – Yom Kippur or the Day of Atonement is the most popular day of fasting followed in Judaism. The Jews also fast on six other days each year including Tish B'Av, which is the day when their temples were destroyed.

Buddhism – Strict forms of fasting (that can potentially lead to starvation and death) are not part of Buddhism, which strongly advocates a 'middle path.' However, in most monasteries, monks eat only one meal a day (around noon time) as a way of staying healthy. Eating only one meal a day aids in meditation.

The average Buddhist fasts on certain days to understand the feeling of hunger, which helps in empathizing with people who don't have enough to eat. Fasting for Buddhism is done moderately in line with their core 'Middle Path' belief.

Christianity – Nearly all Christian sects fast during the 40-day Lent period that precedes Easter Sunday as a form of penitence and self-control. Christians follow various fasting methods including giving up meat, sacrificing certain luxuries, or one-meal-a-day fasting.

Hinduism – Fasting is a critical element of the Hindu religion. Some sects have practically one fasting day each week! There are fortnightly, monthly, and yearly fasting days too. Fasting in Hinduism is rooted in spirituality, health, and self-control and sacrifice.

Jainism – In the Jain religion, fasting is taken very seriously. In fact, even in modern times, many followers of the Jain religion have their last meal before 5 p.m. Additionally, there is a self-starvation ritual in Jainism referred to as 'Santhara' wherein the participant chooses voluntary death by starvation; perhaps, an extreme measure for the contemporary world. However, it reflects the seriousness with which fasting is treated in Jainism.

Islam – Fasting during the month of Ramadan is one of the 'Five Pillars' of the Islamic faith. Ramadan fasting calls for complete and absolute abstinence from food and drinks including water during daylight. You are allowed to eat only after sunset and before sunrise on all the days of the holy month.

Followers of Islam fast because they believe self-control and sacrifice get them closer to God. Moreover, Muslims believe that voluntary abstinence helps one understand and empathize with less fortunate people thereby increasing compassion and love for all mankind.

Interestingly, voluntary fasting was one of the most popular effective non-violent means employed by Mahatma Gandhi to fight for freedom from his country from the British. This great leader literally cajoled the British to leave India voluntary by using fasting methods multiple times to showcase his protest of their rule.

Understanding Breakfast, Lunch, and Dinner

During the ancient civilizations, breakfast was unheard of. The Greeks and Romans ate one meal around noontime not because there was a scarcity of food (these two civilizations thrived) but, because it was believed that eating one meal a day was good for health. Eating more than needed was not a sign of gluttony, thought the ancient wise men.

There is an interesting story to the famous 'bacon and eggs' breakfast that is a big hit in today's world. During the Middle Ages, on Monday and Tuesday preceding Ash Wednesday, people were compelled to exhaust the remains of meat and eggs as these items are not allowed to be consumed during Lent. As pork and bacon were the most commonly used meats in those days, the people then would cook them together which is believed to be the precursor of the modern-day bacon and eggs.

Around the 17th century, the aristocracy and the wealthy started consuming a morning meal, and called it breakfast for 'breaking the fast.' The fast here refers to not eating during the night because you were 'sleeping!' With the advent of the Industrial Revolution, there was an increasing number of workers working in factories putting in standard work hours from morning to night. These workers needed a substantial meal in the morning to sustain them throughout the day. Thus, breakfast began to be consumed by the common people.

John Harvey Kellogg created cornflakes in the beginning of the 20th century and revolutionized and popularized the concept of breakfast, and today, not necessarily for the correct reasons, most people believe that breakfast should never be missed. The explanation for this misplaced belief is explained in the later chapters of this book.

Now, coming to lunch, this meal seemed to always exist in human history though it was not called by the same name. People in nearly all civilizations had their primary meal of the day around noon. During the Industrial Revolution, factory workers toiled for over 6-8 hours at a stretch. The concept of 'luncheon' came into effect at this time, which gave these workers sustenance to carry on their strenuous labor for the rest of the day.

The evening/last meal of the day happened before sunset or before darkness set in. With the invention of artificial lighting, the inclusion of a substantial breakfast and lunch (which kept people not hungry enough for an early dinner), the evening meal got pushed to a later time than before and became the modern-day dinner.

By the end of the 18th century, people fit in three meals a day. This concept was more common in urban areas where factories flourished and working hours were structured and standardized. Therefore, before this period, 3-4 meals were unheard of, and yet people lived healthily. In fact, the concept of stress (which is closely related to food today) was almost absent until the beginning of the Industrial Revolution, which more or less standardized the concept of 'working hours' that stretched into long and laboriously monotonous ones.

Therefore, the intermittent fasting of today is not a new concept. It has been part of human history from ages ago, and we are only trying to give it a contemporary profile aligned with the lifestyle of today. Our ancestors just did the natural thing. We are trying to give a fanciful name, that's it.

Moreover, multiple scientific research studies only seem to reiterate the benefits that our ancestors already knew and took advantage of. The observations and biological inferences from these studies on intermittent fasting enhance our understanding of the way our body behaves for a positive impact; these benefits are not new, they were always there.

Read on, and find out more about how intermittent fasting works, and how you can leverage its multiple benefits including weight loss, improved physical fitness, improved levels of psychical and mental energy, increased resistance to illnesses, and more.

Chapter One: How Does Intermittent Fasting Work and What Are Its Benefits

Let's start understanding this intriguing subject by answer the most pertinent question, "What is intermittent fasting (IF)?"

As already explained in the introduction chapter, before the modern-day trend of having 3-4 meals a day started, our hunter-gatherer ancestors and the wise people of the ancient civilizations had only 1-2 meals. That is nothing but intermittent fasting. Switching between feasting and fasting is called intermittent fasting.

Intermittent fasting is not a diet. It is a pattern or method of eating. The most critical aspect of intermittent fasting is not on WHAT is eaten but WHEN it is eaten.

No major concern exists on micromanaging consumed nutrients as long as you are not overeating during your feeding period. Additionally, while processed and junk foods are to be avoided, all other nutrients including carbs, proteins, fats, etc. are not required to be measured and micromanaged to the last calorie which is what most crash diets expect you to do.

You choose the time of fasting and feasting based on your lifestyle and eating habits. The feasting time is the window in which you can eat your 1-2 meals, and the fasting time is the window when you fast. One of the simplest forms of intermittent fasting commonly used by beginners is to skip breakfast.

So, here's the scene: You have had your dinner at 8 p.m., and you skip breakfast the next day. Don't eat anything until your lunchtime, which is typically 12 noon. So, you have remained in the fasted state from 8 p.m. the previous night until 12 noon the next day which totals to 16 hours, and is known as the 16:8 type of intermittent fasting.

Similarly, there are other types of IF that you can choose from depending on your needs and lifestyle. The types of IF are discussed in Chapter Three.

How Does Intermittent Fasting Work?

Your body can exist only in two states namely fed and fasted states. In the fed state, the level of insulin in your blood rises. Insulin is a critical hormone that plays an important part in digestion. It is produced by the pancreas and is essential for the body to use glucose or sugar from consumed carbs for energy. Insulin is needed to balance the sugar level in your blood and to prevent hyperglycemia (a condition resulting from excessive sugar in the blood) and hypoglycemia (a condition resulting from dangerously low levels of sugar in the blood).

Nearly all the foods we consume except pure fat increase the level of insulin in your blood. Insulin is a nutrient sensor, and 'senses' the ingestion of carb- and protein-containing foods. Very few foods do not increase insulin production and release when they are consumed; pure fat is one such nutrient. On the other extreme, carbohydrates, and specifically processed carbs cause insulin to spike.

Now, your body needs a continuous supply for energy for its basic metabolism. Some of the critical metabolic activities, which require a constant supply of energy, include:

- Pumping of blood by the heart
- Detoxification functions of the liver and kidneys
- The exhalation and inhalation functioning of the lungs
- The functioning of the brain

Therefore, your body needs a supply of energy that is always available, no matter what. As we cannot keep eating all the time, the excess food we have consumed gets converted to energy and gets stored. In the fed state, the energy needed to carry out basic metabolism is taken from the ingested food. In the fasted state, this energy is taken from the stored food.

If you are going to supply your body with newly-ingested food at all times, it is never going to use the energy from the stored food, which is nothing but fat and glycogen stored in the liver (limited amount) and fat as adipose tissue all over the body (unlimited amount).

During intermittent fasting, the supply of energy from the ingested food gets exhausted, and the body is compelled to reach out and take the energy from the stored food, which primarily exists as fat in the body resulting in weight loss and multiple other benefits.

There is no one method of IF that suits everyone. The biggest advantage of using IF is that it is very flexible. You can choose the type that is most suitable for you. You can start with something as simple as fasting for 10-12 hours initially, and when your body gets adjusted to the new metabolism, then you can gradually increase the intensity by increasing the duration of the fasting window.

Understanding Human Metabolism

We need to understand human metabolism in a little more detail to know how IF benefits us immensely. Nearly all our foods are a combination of three macronutrients namely carbohydrates, proteins, and fats.

The foods we eat have these macronutrients in varying compositions. While some foods such as rice, pasta, bread, potato, and others have a higher percentage of carbs, some other foods such as legumes, lean meats, etc. have a higher amount of proteins, and some others such as red meats, oils, etc. have high amounts of fats.

The process of metabolism begins when we start consuming food. It starts with the breakdown of macronutrients into its component parts, and continues until the energy released is either used up or stored in the body. Carbohydrates get converted to glucose or simple sugar. Proteins are broken down into amino acids. Fats become fatty acids and glycerol. These components are further converted into energy for immediate needs, and the excess amounts are stored as energy reserves in various parts of the body. Here is a short summary of what happens to each component parts of each of the macronutrients during metabolism:

Glucose – After a meal, the blood glucose level quickly rises resulting in the production of insulin. Insulin transfers the glucose from the blood to the cells, tissues, and muscles of your body where it is used for energy. The glucose that is not immediately required gets converted into glycogen and is in your muscles and liver. However, the amount of glycogen that can be stored in these two places is limited, and, therefore, any glucose in excess of this amount gets converted to fat and is stored as adipose tissues all over your body. Typically, glucose is the primary source of fuel for your body.

Amino acids – Amino acids are the end-products of protein metabolism. They are needed for repair and maintenance of cells and tissues. Amino acids are also necessary for the synthesis of new cells. The normal adult body needs very few amino acids for repair and maintenance. Therefore, the excess is converted into glucose by the liver which again goes through the process of getting stored as glycogen in the liver and muscle, and when the glycogen accumulation level is breached, it gets converted into fat and is stored as adipose tissue all over the body.

Fatty acids – It is highly unlikely that fatty acids from fats will be needed for immediate use as most of the energy needed for basic metabolism is obtained from the glucose of the supplied food (especially during fed state). Some amount of fatty acids along with amino acids are used for repair and maintenance. Therefore, the fatty acids get converted to fats and stored in adipose tissue as stored energy for use when energy from the fed state is exhausted completely.

For several hours after eating, your body is busy converting all the excess food you have eaten into stored energy for later use. This is the fed state. When the storage process is completed, then your body gets into the fasted state, and at the beginning of this state, your fuel stores do not get any added fuel. Instead, fuel from this stored energy is used up by the body.

The longer you put your body in the fasted state, the more fuel from the stored energy is used up releasing the fat loss.

A Scientific Explanation of Intermittent Fasting

The body's energy sources come in the form of glucose and fats. Glucose is easier to burn than fat and, therefore, in a fed state (when there is a continuous supply of glucose from the consumed food), the body chooses to burn sugars for its energy needs instead of fat. Fats along with excess amino acids and glucose get stored as adipose or fat tissues for use in the absence of glucose.

Primarily, intermittent fasting drives your body to access the energy needed for its requirements from stored fat because you have deliberately cut off the supply of food that would otherwise have come from the 3-4 meals consumed each day. Stored fat is nothing but fuel energy that can be used by the body when its default 'preferred' form of fuel (typically glucose or sugar) is not available.

Again, excess energy from consumed food is stored in two ways in the body. First, excess glucose gets converted to glycogen and is kept in the liver and muscles. These places have limited amounts of storage space, like your refrigerator. Storing and accessible energy in this 'refrigerator' is easy.

But, because of the limited space, the body cannot store much here. Therefore, any additional energy in the form of glucose or amino acids or fatty acids get converted into fats and stored in adipose tissues all over the body. The body is similar to a large-sized industrial-grade freezer, which can store humongous amounts of food energy. Storing this kind of food energy is difficult, and accessing it is even more difficult.

So, to summarize, stored energy in your body is available in two forms; the easily accessible but limited amount of glycogen in the liver and muscles, and the not-so-easily accessible but an unlimited supply of fat in the adipose tissues.

During the fasting state, the blood-insulin levels fall triggering the body to reach out for stored energy for its fuel needs because there is no energy supply from consumed food. So, the body will first reach out for glycogen from the liver and muscles. On sustained fasting, this limited supply of glycogen will also be exhausted, and that is when the body reaches out to stored fat for its energy supply.

It takes at least 12 hours of being in the fasting state for the body to use a significant amount of fat for its energy needs. The longer you extend the fasting window, the more energy is used up by the body from the stored fat cells. Exercising and remaining physically active during the fasting state helps to increase the rate of fat burn.

Some people are more prone to get into the fat-burning mode faster and more effectively than others. This biological tendency is referred to as 'metabolic flexibility.' The good thing about 'metabolic flexibility' is that it works like a muscle; the more you work at it, the more flexible and stronger it will become. Therefore, after a few weeks of practicing intermittent fasting, your body's metabolic flexibility will increase, and you will be able to burn fat faster and more effectively than before.

In the fasting state, the body uses a combination of the following forms of fuel for all its energy purposes:

- Fatty acids that are released from adipose tissues or body fat
- Ketones from the fatty acids produced by the liver
- Glucose from glycogen

So, why does the body need this combination of fuel sources? Because different physiological and biological functions performed by different organs and tissues need different kinds of fuels for optimal functioning. Here are a few examples:

- Muscles can use energy from fatty acids or glucose obtained from their stored glycogen to work efficiently.

- The heart works efficiently with energy from fatty acids.

- Nerves and the brain typically need glucose energy for optimal functioning; they can also work well with ketones.

- RBCs or red blood cells can work only with energy from glucose.

Even in the fasting state, your body's excellent energy mechanism can maintain sufficient levels of blood-glucose for RBCs to perform at their peak levels. The brain can extract glucose from glycogen through glycogenolysis, and the liver can synthesize new glucose molecules by breaking down stored fats and amino acids.

Difference between Intermittent Fasting and Starvation

One of the most significant misconceptions about intermittent fasting is that it is likened to starvation. Even those who are keenly interested in giving it a try are worried that they will get into starvation mode in which muscle gets converted into energy resulting in muscle loss. Here are some myth-busting points that will help you understand the difference better:

Myth #1 – Why does our store the excess food as fat? – So as to use this stored energy during times of food shortage. Let us use the example of our hunter-gatherer ancestors again. During summers, they got a lot of food, ate well, and become healthier. Going out to hunt during winters was foolhardy, and so our wise ancestors stayed indoors with little or no access to food resulting in voluntary fasting.

How did they survive these winters then? Their bodies used up the stored fats for energy needs. If during fasting, muscles were used instead of fat, our ancestors would have had round tummies and thin hands and legs, right? This was not the case. Moreover, why would our body store fat for future use, and use up muscle when the time comes? This argument is quite contrary to the way nature works. Therefore, muscles do not waste away during fasting.

When all the fat has been used up by the body, and even then there was no food, it would reach out into muscles for its energy needs, but not until then.

Myth #2 – Muscles are the first energy reserves that our body uses in the absence of food – To understand this, we need to understand why our body builds muscles. Muscles are built and maintained for strength. Let us go back to our ancestors. If muscles instead of fat were broken down for regular energy needs, then our ancestors would not have had the strength to survive the winter, and come out at the other end, ready for a new kill so that their families could get food. Using up muscles weakens the body, which is against the natural survival instinct of all living beings.

So, let us end this argument with the following basic difference between starvation and fasting:

- Fasting is the voluntary abstinence of foods during which our body uses stored fat for its energy needs. There is no lack of essential nutrients to do normal work.

- Starvation, on the other hand, is a state when essential nutrients needed to support life.

Benefits of Intermittent Fasting

Now, that you know how naturally intermittent fasting works, let us look at some of its benefits.

Weight Loss

Although Chapter Five talks about weight loss in a bit more detail, as this is one of the biggest benefits of IF, it would be unfair not to mention it (at least briefly) in this section. Fasting ensures your source of glucose is completely drained out so that your body switches into fat-burning mode resulting in effective weight loss. Moreover, studies proved that an occasional brief break from intermittent fasting does not really impact your progress negatively.

The best part of weight loss from intermittent fasting is that your belly fat is reduced considerably. When your body burns fat, it reaches out to all parts for stored fat including the adamant belly fat. Thus, if you sustain your efforts at intermittent fasting, your belly fat will also dissolve.

Reduces Insulin Resistance

One of the most common diseases of modern times is Type 2 diabetes, which is characterized by increased insulin resistance. Therefore, any therapy that reduces the level of insulin in the blood can help in controlling type 2 diabetes. Intermittent fasting is known to impact insulin resistance positively thereby reducing the risk of Type 2 diabetes. Some studies revealed that men were more likely to be benefited than women.

Reduces Inflammation and Oxidative Stress

Oxidative stress is characterized by the presence of harmful free radicals that are unstable and can react with and damage other critical molecules in the body such as proteins and DNA. Based on various scientific studies, experts opine that intermittent fasting improves the body's resistance to oxidative stress, which, in turn, reduces the risk of multiple diseases and illnesses caused by oxidative stress.

Additionally, intermittent fasting is also known the increase the body's capability to fight against inflammation, a huge risk factor for many common disorders. Reduced oxidative stress and the decrease of chronic inflammation from intermittent fasting can also improve the texture of your skin as damaging free radicals become less than before. This also helps to clear acne and pimples from your face.

Improves Brain Functioning

Advancing age restricts blood flow to the brain resulting in the shrinkage of neurons and reduction in brain volume. IF stems the process of aging, and keeps you mentally alert and sharp. Here are some ways that IF boosts your brain functioning:

Promotes autophagy and prevents degeneration of neurons – Intermittent fasting promotes autophagy in the brain. Autophagy is the body's natural process to clean out damaged cells and replace them with newly generated cells. IF promotes autophagy specifically in the neurons of the brain thereby facilitating improved defense against brain-related disorders. IF protects neurons from degeneration and death. IF is known to help guard neurons found in the brain from neuronal death or excitotoxic stress.

Lowers risk of multiple diseases – IF promotes brain health and thereby reduces the risk of brain-related disorders such as Parkinson's and Alzheimer's. Moreover, intermittent fasting helps in weight reduction and therefore facilitates reduced obesity, and helps in fighting against diabetes; both these conditions increase the risk of Alzheimer's.

Reduces depression – Multiple studies have revealed that when people suffering from depression resorted to intermittent fasting, there was a marked improvement in their moods, calmness and mental alertness.

Boosts memory – Studies have proven that IF helps to boost learning and memory, which, in turn, helps, protect the brain against severe neurodegenerative diseases.

Improves Heart Health

Intermittent fasting has shown to improve heart health by positively impacting and regulating multiple risk factors associated with heart disease including LDL and total cholesterol, blood pressure, inflammatory markers, blood triglycerides, and, of course, blood sugar levels.

Promotes Longevity

In addition to reducing insulin resistance, lowering cholesterol levels, and improving brain functioning (all of which contribute to improving longevity), intermittent fasting also reduces the risk of the following deadly diseases and risk factors resulting in improved longevity:

Slows down cancer growth – Multiple studies have revealed that when intermittent fasting is done in combination with chemotherapy, then the progression of skin cancer and breast cancer can be slowed down. This happens because IF is believed to enhance lymphocytes that attack and kill cancer cells.

Slows down the aging process – By reducing oxidative stress and inflammation, intermittent fasting is known to slow down the aging process thereby enhancing longevity. Intermittent fasting is known to manipulate the cellular power generators or the mitochondrial network. These mitochondria were observed to be fused together in study participants who were doing intermittent fasting. Fusing together helped increase the power of the mitochondrial network resulting in their improved productivity and efficiency. This meant that cells got increased energy and became vibrant which, in turn, resulting in improved health and slowing down of the aging process.

Improves Energy and Productivity

Overeating and eating excessive refined foods make us tired and weak. Ask yourself how you feel after a heavy meal. Sleepy, tired, and completely unenergetic, right? That is what overconsumption of food does to your body. Fasting, on the other hand, keeps your mind alert and sharp and improves your powers of focus and concentration.

What happens during fasting is this. The digestive system does not need any energy as there is no food for it to work on. Therefore, this energy is 'freed up' and is used for other productive work by your body including improving brain function, repair and maintenance of cells and tissues, etc.

Improved brain function translates into enhanced cognitive powers thereby rendering you more alert and capable of greater mental accuracy. Fasting also makes you feel lighter and more energetic because, during fasting, your body gets its energy from fat and not glucose. One gram of fat releases 9 calories as against 4 calories from one gram of glucose. Therefore, your energy levels go up with intermittent fasting.

Additionally, intermittent fasting increases the production and release of growth hormone. This hormone is vital for the preservation of muscle mass and bone density. It also helps in promoting fat metabolism and is also needed for cell growth and repair. Growth hormone production reduces with advancing age. Intermittent fasting is believed to be one of the most effective ways to triggering the production of this critical hormone.

Improved Taste Sensitivity

Eating salty, sugary, and processed foods desensitize our taste buds to the subtle flavors of natural, wholesome foods. Our taste buds are used to excessive flavors and lose the ability to identify natural flavors. After a couple of fasting periods, your taste buds functions are reset to their natural levels, and you will be able to appreciate and savor earthy, wholesome, and subtle flavors. In fact, after some weeks into intermittent fasting, you could find yourself becoming allergic to overpowering flavors like those found in junk and processed foods.

Simplifies Your Life

And finally, intermittent fasting simplifies your life because you don't need to worry about your meals as often as before. You just have to plan for 2 slightly large meals, and one little snack. In fact, after you have gained experience with IF, and extend your fasting window even more than before, you will notice you have a lot of time in your hands as meal-planning, spending time eating your meals, and other food and cooking related activities reduce time considerably. Your life becomes simple, easy, and free, leaving you more time and energy to do the things you love.

Improved Willpower and Self-Confidence

Intermittent fasting calls for strong willpower to battle against ever-assailing food temptations that surround you. Moreover, you need strong willpower to fight against hunger pangs, cravings and other psychological temptations as well. With each battle, the strength of your willpower improves, and you find it increasingly easy to resist temptations of all kinds and be disciplined to your IF cause.

When you notice the tangible results of this increased willpower in the form of compliments from friends and family on your weight loss, on the improvement of your skin texture, increased energy, etc. your level of self-confidence also goes up. You enjoy the victory of surmounting multiple challenges that you encounter to achieve your goal successfully. This self-confidence spreads to other personal and professional aspects of your life too.

Chapter Two: Some Myths Busted and Who Should Avoid Intermittent Fasting

There are multiple misconceived and unsubstantiated myths floating around regarding intermittent fasting. Before we go further, it makes sense to bust some of these myths, and also let you know some contraindications and precautions that need to be taken for certain individuals. So, let's go bust some myths:

Myth #1 – Breakfast Is the Most Important and Un-missable Meal of the Day

Most of us have been brainwashed into believing that breakfast is the most important meal of the day and that without it, you are going to feel fatigued resulting in unproductivity, inefficiency, and also, bingeing during lunch time. This advice is quite misplaced.

When you wake up in the morning, your body has just about reached the fasted state (after nearly 10-12 hours after the last meal). Insulin and glucose levels are low, and your body has begun to reach out to stored fat for its energy needs. Now, when you eat breakfast, your fat-burning comes to an immediate halt, which is counterproductive to weight loss, and multiple other benefits of IF. Instead, if you simply skipped your morning breakfast, then your body will go into an intense fat-burning state.

Eating a high-carb breakfast is the worst scenario because both insulin and glucose levels will spike, and your body will get out of the fasted state almost immediately. Not only does eating breakfast spike insulin and glucose levels, and shut off the fat-burning process but also a lot more needless calories get accumulated as fat again. Additionally, later on during the morning, you will see huge drops in glucose levels, which is the perfect trigger for hunger resulting in increased cravings.

As your body gets into the fat-burning mode faster and more effectively than before, you will notice that you hardly get hungry in the mornings. You also don't feel any kind of excessive cravings before your lunchtime, and yet you will have adequate energy to perform all your activities efficiently and productively. Our ancestors, wittingly or unwittingly, followed this exact lifestyle. They went out early in the morning (on an empty stomach) to hunt for food and gather wild berries, and came back home in the late afternoon or early evening to eat one big satiating meal of the day!

So, the idea that skipping breakfast is bad for health is a myth because the biological processes confirm quite the opposite. In fact, multiple research studies have revealed results that counter earlier observations that eating breakfast is good for obesity reduction. Therefore, as a beginner in intermittent fasting, skipping breakfast is one of the easiest and most effective ways to begin your IF journey as a large portion of the fasting window is covered during your sleep time.

Myth #2 - Intermittent Fasting Results in Low Blood-Sugar of Hypoglycemia

Multiple studies have proven that normal individuals who are not suffering from any ailments and who are not taking medication for diabetes can fast for long periods of time without any negative impact on blood-sugar levels. In fact, in nearly all non-diabetics, it is seen that hypoglycemia sets in when excessive carbs are consumed. Here is what happens when high-carb foods are consumed frequently:

- Blood-glucose spikes

- Blood-insulin spikes

- Blood-glucose drops significantly (hypoglycemia sets in) after some time while insulin remains at more or less the same level

- Cravings set in driving you to eat more

Diabetics on medication will have to necessarily check with their physicians before starting off intermittent fasting.

Myth #3 - Intermittent Fasting Slows Down Metabolism

This is also a complete myth. Multiple studies have shown that there is no effect on metabolism even when fasting is carried out for 72 hours. On the contrary, fasting could marginally increase metabolism driven by the increased release of catecholamines such as adrenaline or epinephrine, dopamine, and norepinephrine.

Further, fasting activates the sympathetic nervous system that is known for fight/flight response; another key element to increase metabolism. And this makes a lot of sense because our hunter-gatherer ancestors needed the fight-flight response to work at its peak when they hunted, and the 'rest and digest' (driven by the parasympathetic nerves) mode activated at night.

Therefore, IF slowing down metabolism is wrong.

Myth #4 - Intermittent Fasting Leads to Muscle Loss

Another common misconception about intermittent fasting is that people think they will lose muscle when they fast. However, nothing is further from the truth because the growth hormone level is significantly increased during fasted states. Studies have shown that growth hormone rises nearly 2000% after 24 hours of fasting.

So, why is growth hormone significant for muscle? Because it is anabolic, which means it, builds muscles. Bodybuilders combine growth hormone with testosterone in their health drinks to result in the dual advantage of building muscle and losing fat. The level of growth hormone increases during fast to facilitate muscle preservation.

It is for this reason that our hunter-gatherer ancestors (who were driven to fasting because of a shortage of food) became stronger with each generation. If fasting made you weaker, human beings would not have survived and thrived for so many millennia.

Not only is muscle preserved during fasting but if combined with strength training, muscles can even grow. Also, during fasting, our alertness levels are very high driven by the release of epinephrine and norepinephrine.

Myth #5 – Eating Small Meals Frequently Is Healthy Whereas Eating Fewer Large-Sized Meals Is Not

Eating frequent small meals is believed to keep the metabolism going, and keeping your body is a fasting or starvation mode reduces metabolism. This is a complete myth. Fat burning is what increasing metabolism, and to burn fat, you must remain in the fasted state for a long time.

The more frequently you feed your body, the less time it will remain in a fasted state. In fact, if your meals are very frequent, no matter who small your meals are, your body will always have access to glucose for its energy, and will never reach out to its stored fat for its energy needs.

The more frequent your meals, the less efficient your body will be when it comes to burning fat. The longer the duration of fasting state, the more efficient your body becomes in burning fat. Additionally, we have been told that proteins need to be supplied to the body through frequent meals. This idea has no scientific basis. Yes, an adequate amount of proteins is needed for healthy muscles. However, there is no requirement for frequent supply of this nutrient.

Who can benefit from intermittent fasting? Nearly anyone and everyone can benefit from the intermittent fasting. Here is a short summary of the benefits of IF discussed in Chapter One, and a few more:

- Promotes fat and weight loss
- Enhances insulin sensitivity
- Improves metabolism
- Promotes longevity
- Improves brain functioning
- Reduces risks of neurodegenerative diseases
- Increased resistance to hunger pangs
- Improves your ability to appreciate wholesome foods
- Improves eating patterns

- Rests the digestive system

If you want to leverage the above benefits and more, you can start intermittent fasting by choosing the method that is most suitable for you. However, there are a few contraindications and precautions for certain individuals. In fact, for certain people, IF is strictly forbidden. Here are a few examples of people who should avoid intermittent fasting unless prescribed by a qualified physician.

Who Should Not Try Intermittent Fasting?

- Pregnant women and lactating mothers; they need extra energy and, therefore, experimenting with intermittent fasting at this time is prohibited for health reasons.

- People with a history of eating disorders; for such people, it is important to set their eating patterns in order first, and then jump into intermittent fasting.

- People suffering from chronic stress; in the initial days of intermittent fasting, there could be some amount of stress considering the change in lifestyle that you are adopting. Therefore, people with chronic stress issues could end up complicating their problems even further and should avoid IF.

- People with insomnia issues. Insomnia also creates a lot of stress, and IF should be avoided for the same reasons as for people with chronic stress.

Other than the above set of people, typically, intermittent fasting can be tried by everyone else. However, it is always a good thing to speak to a qualified physician, and take his or her opinion to ensure you are doing the right thing for you.

Chapter Three: Methods of Intermittent Fasting

As you know by now that intermittent fasting involves abstaining from eating for predetermined periods of time alternated with periods of eating. The duration when you don't eat is called the fasting window, and the duration when you eat is called the eating window.

One of the biggest advantages of intermittent fasting is that there are multiple variations available, and you can choose what suits you the best. So, let us look at some of the methods of intermittent fasting along with critical research observations for each of them.

Intermittent Fasting #1: Random Meal Skipping

This method is great for beginners where you simply choose to randomly skip meals depending on the intensity of your hunger or time restraints or any other reason. Again, it is important not to overeat at the next meal.

This method is likely to be successful for people who monitor their hunger pangs and respond appropriately to them. Such people eat when they are hungry, and skip meals when they are not hungry. For some people, this appears to be a more natural method of intermittent fasting than the others. There is no formal pattern to be followed.

Intermittent Fasting #2: 12:12 Method - 12-Hour Fasting Window and 12-Hour Eating Window

This is, perhaps, the simplest and easiest method for beginners to take their first step into the world of intermittent fasting. In this method, you can choose two fixed 12-hour periods for eating and fasting. Some research studies have observed that the body begins to burn fat after fasting for 10-16 hours.

Therefore, fasting for 12 hours can potentially give the body a 2-hour window for fat-burning. Some studies have proven the efficacy of this intermittent fasting method in weight loss. The reason why this method is great for beginners is that the fasting duration is relatively small (only 12 hours) out of which about 6-8 hours coincide with your sleeping time; if the fasting duration is chosen sensibly. In this method, the beginner can eat the same amount of calories as before.

For example, you can choose the fasting window to be between 8 p.m. and 8 a.m. So, ensure you finish your dinner before 8 in the evening, and have your breakfast after 8 the next morning. The other meals of the day can remain the same for you.

For many beginners, this would be a perfect way to start because prior to this, the fasting window would ideally have been between 8 and 10 hours. For example, typically, most of us (who are not into IF) have our dinner at around 10 p.m., and the next meal would be breakfast at around 8 a.m. leaving a fasting window of 10 hours. With the 12-hour IF method, you would only need to extend the fasting time by 2 hours which is not very difficult to do.

Once your body and mind get used to the concept of fasting, then you can extend the fasting window to the next method, which is 16:8 method.

Pros – It is very easy to follow this method as you only need to extend your fasting period by a couple of hours.

Cons – The beneficial effects of IF may not show through this method because fat-burning is restricted to only 2 hours.

Intermittent Fasting #3: 16:8 Method – 16-Hour Fasting Window and 8-Hour Eating Window

This method is called the Leangains Method where you fast for 16 hours (for men) and 14 hours (for women) at a stretch and eat in the remaining 8-10-hour window. You can move into this method after you have tried the 12:12 option and found that either it did not work for you or it worked for some time, and now you have plateaued.

Typically in this method, you should finish your dinner before 8 p.m., skip breakfast the next morning, and eat your lunch, which will be the first meal of the day. Multiple studies conducted on mice using this method revealed great results in the fight against obesity, and protection against liver disease, diabetes and inflammation.

Skipping breakfast is not bad for your health. The myth surrounding breakfast was broken down in Chapter Two. Here are some more great reasons why missing breakfast is actually a good thing:

Skipping breakfast does not affect your metabolism negatively – Studies have shown that missing out on breakfast does not slow down your metabolism. Metabolism is driven by physical activity, the base metabolic rate, and the energy used to digest food. Metabolism is a continuous process that takes place 24/7 and does not depend on any meal. Therefore, if you are eating breakfast in the morning only on the assumption that otherwise, your metabolism will suffer, you can stop right now.

Eating breakfast does not aid weight loss – In multiple studies, it was observed that weight loss was affected by eating breakfast. The people who ate breakfast lost weight to the same extent as people who skipped breakfast with other factors remaining common.

Your brain continues to work efficiently even if there is no food in your stomach – It is a common misconception that not having food in the stomach reduces the efficiency of the brain. Our brain is too sophisticated an organ to depend on food in the stomach for its functioning. There are multiple other energy sources it draws its needed calories from for its efficient functioning. Therefore, there is no need to fill up your empty stomach with breakfast as soon as you wake up.

Skipping breakfast is not essential for the 16:8 method. You can choose to eat your dinner or your last meal of the day at 4 p.m., which will also give you the same, 16:8 fasting and feasting windows. Sugarless coffee, tea, and other calorie-free drinks are fine in the fasting window. A bit of milk in your coffee and tea is fine too. This method is easily adaptable into any kind of lifestyle. The trick is to keep the feeding window consistent to prevent hormones from being unbalanced.

Pros – It is easy to maintain this method because you can eat whenever you want during the 8-hour feeding window. Most people prefer breaking their nutritional requirements into three different meals in the 8-hour window.

Cons – You can eat whenever you want during the 8-hour eating window. However, there are some fairly strict guidelines as to what you can and what you cannot eat for this method, especially if you are working out. Moreover, if you eat three meals in 8 hours, then it is quite likely to consume more calories than needed; a situation, which is counterproductive to weight loss. It requires you to maintain a strict eye over what you eat in this method.

Intermittent Fasting #4: 5:2 Method – Fast for Two Days, and Eat Normally for 5 Days of the Week

The 5:2 intermittent fasting method also called the Fast Diet works like this:

- Men eat 600 calories, and women consume 500 calories on 2 days of the week

- Eat normally on 5 days of the week

The reduced calorie intake on the two days can potentially result in a lot of fat loss. However, it is imperative that you don't binge-eat on the normal-feeding days. There should be at least a one-day gap between the two fasting days. Here is an example:

- Reduced calorie intake on Mondays and Thursdays
- Normal calorie intake on the other days

You can choose any two days of your convenience. You only have to remember to keep a gap of one day between the two days when calorie-restriction is enforced. Also, it is important that normal eating days does not mean you can eat anything and everything you want. You must eat as if you didn't fast at all.

Moreover, the choice of foods for IF, although not restricted excessively unlike other diets, play an important part for success. Chapter Six discusses the foods that should be avoided and to be included in IF.

Some studies focused on the 5:2 method showed that it was possible to control obesity to the same extent in this way as by restricting calorie intake continuously.

Pros – You will have to restrict food intake only on two days and this can be easier to maintain than having to fast continuously on all days even if it is only for 16 hours.

Cons – Some people could find it difficult to work normally with only 500-600 calorie intake.

Intermittent Fasting #5: The Eat-Stop-Eat Method – Fasting for 24 Hours Once or Twice Every Week

This method calls for complete fasting for 24 hours at a stretch to be done once or twice a week. People fast from dinner to dinner or breakfast to breakfast or lunch to lunch giving their digestive systems a break for 24 hours. You can choose the 24-hour slot as per your needs and comfort levels. During the 24 hours, you cannot consume any foods though liquids in the form of sugar-free tea, coffee, water, and other calorie-free beverages are allowed.

On the non-fasting days, you can eat normally remembering to consume food as if you did not fast. Binge-eating after the day of a fast defeats the very purpose of fasting. So, you reduce the total calorie intake for the week while having the freedom to consume what you normally like.

Pros – Yes, for some of us, 24 hours might seem like a long period to stay without food. However, you don't have to start with 24 hours. Begin the fasting day with the intention of staying off food for 24 hours. Try and fast for as long as you feel comfortable in the initial stages. Increase the duration of your fasting period gradually over time until you reach the maximum 24 hours. Therefore, the biggest advantage of this method lies in its flexibility. Start slow and increase in small bouts.

Another great thing about the Fast Diet is that there are really no 'forbidden foods.' You can eat what you love to eat providing you don't make up for the fasting day calorie loss.

Cons – In the initial days, fasting for 24 hours could be a stretch for some people. They usually cite reasons like fatigues, headaches, crankiness, irritation, etc., and typically give up without much resistance. Initial periods of uneasiness are expected when you start your intermittent fasting journey. However, these discomforts are temporary in nature and disappear once your body gets accustomed to the new eating pattern.

Additionally, the long fasting period also enhances people's temptations to binge-eat after its completion. A lot of self-control is needed to eat only the normal amount of food after fasting for 24 hours, which could be a huge challenge for many.

Intermittent Fasting #6: The 18:6 Method – Fasting for 18 Hours and Feeding for 6 Hours

Once you are comfortable with the 16:8 method, you can slowly increase your fasting period to 18 hours. This is typically the best form of intermittent fasting to achieve for beginners. The fat burning state exists for about 6-8 hours resulting in optimum lipolysis efficiency.

Like the 16:8 method, this type also calls for skipping breakfast, a light lunch at around noon, a little snack at 3 p.m., and dinner (the last meal of the day at 6 in the evening) which will leave you a fasting period of 18 hours until the next day's lunch. A major difference between the 16:8 and 18:6 methods is an early dinner, typically not later than 6 p.m. Move to this method from the 16:8 method if you have plateaued there, and you are bound to see some great benefits.

Pros and Cons for the 18:6 method are the same as the 16:8 method except that it might be a struggle (at least initially) to fast for 18 hours a stretch. But, once your body gets used to it, you can keep this pattern of eating for the rest of your life to achieve weight loss and leverage the other IF benefits optimally.

Intermittent Fasting #7 – The Warrior Diet – Fasting for 20 Hours and Feeding for 4 Hours

This is perfect for you once you have perfected the art of intermittent fasting, and your body and mind are ready to take on the extreme challenge. The Warrior Diet calls for a fasting period of 20 hours and a feeding window of 4 hours with a large meal at night. This method also requires you to watch what you eat and when you eat. The concept behind the Warrior Diet is that the human species consists of nocturnal eaters or those whose bodies are naturally programmed to eat one large meal at night. This method, therefore, is designed to align with our body's circadian rhythm.

The fasting window in this method actually translates to eating very little and can include small servings of raw vegetables, fruit, fresh fruit juices, and pure protein foods. All these foods are known to optimize the working of the sympathetic nervous system (responsible for the fight/flight mode), which, in turn, increases our sharpness and alertness, promotes burning of fat, and boosts energy requirements during the day.

The 4-hour eating window closer to dinnertime is designed to activate the parasympathetic nervous system (responsible for rest and relaxation) promoting calmness, efficient digestion and nutrient absorption, and relaxation while allowing the body to use the nutrients for repair, growth and maintenance of cells and tissues.

Eating during the 4-hour feeding window also has a method to be followed. You have to start with vegetables followed by proteins, and then fat. After finishing all these nutrient groups if you are still hungry, then you can add on some amount of carbs.

Pros – One of the most significant pros of the Warrior Diet is that it allows for small snacking (of course, restricted to raw fruit and veggies) thereby making it easier to go through the 20-hour fasting period. There is undoubtedly increased energy levels and a significant amount of fat burning that takes place in your body when you follow this method of intermittent fasting.

Cons – Although small snacks in the form of raw fruit and vegetables and fresh fruit juices are allowed, it can be quite challenging for many people to stay away from conventional food for such a long duration of time. That's why it's called a Warrior Diet; it's only doable by warriors of the intermittent fasting world. Yet, if you do manage to achieve this status, then this method is one of the most effective methods of fat loss and muscle building.

Intermittent Fasting #8 – Alternate Day Fasting

So, you fast one day and eat normally on the next day. Alternate eating and fasting days. This method of intermittent fasting has two variations. In one, people do not eat any solid food on the fasting day and eat as much as they want on the feeding day. In the second variation, people choose to restrict their calorie intake to 500 (for women) and 600 (for men) on the fasting days and eat normally on the feeding days.

Studies have shown that this method of IF is very effective for weight loss and improved heart health. This is quite an extreme form of fasting and may not be suitable for beginners and people with certain medical conditions. Yet, if weight loss is your goal, then this is the most efficient form to follow.

This method is ideal to try out carb cycling for effective carb management. What is carb cycling? It is a relatively new but effective dietary approach where you intentionally vary your carbohydrate intake so that some days are low-carb days and some are high-carb days.

In our efforts to reduce carbohydrate intake, many of us lose out on the multiple benefits of this important macronutrient. Excessive restriction of carbs can lead to reduced metabolism and hormonal imbalance. This is especially crucial for women for whom hormonal imbalances can result in weight loss plateauing. During such times, and to ensure you get a healthy dose of carbs into your system, carb cycling can be used.

In this method, for example, you can have one feeding day as a high-carb day, and the next feeding day as a low-carb day. Please note that carb cycling can also be done on a daily basis. For example, in the 16:8

method, you can choose one high-carb meal while the remaining one or two are low-carb meals. Carb cycling can also weekly or monthly too.

The benefit of carb cycling is that you allow your body to get sufficient supply of this important nutrient, and yet manage to keep carb consumption in check.

Pros – As already mentioned, it is most suited for you if weight loss is your main goal. If you can cut down weekly calorie intake by 20-35%, then you can potentially lose up to 2.5 pounds each week!

Cons – It is an extreme form of IF not because it is not easy to fast on fasting day but because it is quite easy to binge-eat on normal days repeatedly resulting in weight gain instead of weight loss. It is a tricky form to follow. The best ways to ensure you don't binge-eat on normal days is to have meals planned ahead so that you know what you will eat, and stick to that more strictly than if you didn't have a meal plan in place.

Choose your style of intermittent fasting, and most importantly, remember to take it gradually.

Some Self-Assessment Questions Before You Plunge In?

Q1. *Do you get irritable and angry when you are hungry?*

If the answer to the above question is a yes, then maybe, intermittent fasting is not really for you. If you are irritable when you are hungry, then IF might be a bad idea not just for you but for those around you as well. You might want to start really slowly by skipping random meals (especially when you are not hungry), and when you have learned to manage your hunger pangs better, then you can move on to the more difficult methods. If you realize you cannot manage your hunger-triggered anger, then it is best to avoid IF.

Q2. *Do you use cheat meals to stay on course?*

If the answer to this is a yes, then intermittent fasting will work really well for you. For example, if an ice-cream treat on the normal eating day is sufficient to prevent you from eating on the fasting day of the alternate day method, and IF is your cup of tea. Because IF is nothing but cutting down calories on certain days and eating your normal foods on other days. Yet, it makes sense to remind you that feeding days cannot be 'binge-eating' days, especially on unhealthy and processed foods. Then, you are bound to put on weight instead of losing weight!

Q3. Have you checked with your doctor?

While intermittent fasting is relatively safe because it is the most natural thing to do (after all, we are fasting when we sleep every night), sudden long periods of fasting can send your physiological system into a shock, especially if you have an underlying medical condition. Therefore, it is wise to speak to your physician or at least let him know about your plan before you get in. Please reread Chapter Two to know who should avoid IF.

Q4. Do you have an eating disorder?

Intermittent fasting helps you become more appreciative of wholesome foods as fasting periods will allow you saturated (with excessive flavors of processed foods) taste buds to regain some of their lost ability to discern and enjoy subtle flavors. Therefore, it is easy to plan and consume healthy balanced meals between fasting periods for optimum benefit. However, if you have an eating disorder already in place, then intermittent fasting could exacerbate your problems. It is best to avoid it.

Reread the different methods of intermittent fasting, the pros and cons and ask yourself some basic questions, ensure you do not belong to the set of people for whom IF is not recommended, and then take the plunge, and enjoy the benefits of intermittent fasting.

Chapter Four: Tips to Start off, what to Expect in the Initial Days and How to Manage Them

Tips Before You Start Off

Before you start off on your intermittent journey, ready your body and mind with the following tips:

Build your knowledge levels – Remember you will not die if you fast for a few hours. No one can die considering that the human body will is filled with reserve energy to help us survive for up to 30 days even if we did not consume even an ounce of food. Arm yourself with all the required information as to what will happen in your body, how the body will react and behave in the absence of food consumption, and other relevant information.

Read up books like this one, a lot of articles that answer any specific query you may have, and ask people who have used this form of diet and found success. Gather as much information as you can about intermittent fasting. Knowledge is power and armed with this power, you will not feel fear or any kind of burden when you undergo certain expected discomforts at the beginning of your IF journey.

If you start with a closed mind or an antagonistic feeling towards IF, your body and mind are going to resist all your efforts, and it will end in failure.

Feast before your fasting period – Suppose you have chosen to use the 16:8 fasting method and your last meal of the day is going to be at 8 p.m. after which you will be on a 16-hour fasting period. Ensure you have a nutritious and satiating meal at 8 p.m. In fact, eat enough for that 'I'm not going to ever eat a meal again,' feeling to arise in your mind. That way, your hunger pangs will be at bay for a significant portion of the fasting period. Moreover, when you complete the first day of your fasting regimen successfully, you will be motivated to make a success of all the days thereafter.

Be active during the fasting window – One of the biggest causes of excessive eating is boredom and the 'nothing to do' feeling. Therefore, make sure you have something productive to do and keep your mind occupied during the fasting period. This way, you will not feel hunger pangs, and also will be distracted enough not to worry about food. Moreover, finding an activity you love doing will enhance the joy of fasting, and your mind is occupied productively elsewhere.

Combine fasting with low-intensity physical activity – Mild exercises and low-intensity physical activity combine extremely well with intermittent fasting and increase lipolysis or fat burning in your body resulting in more weight loss than without exercises. If you lie around lethargically saying that you are fasting, then making a success of your intermittent fasting endeavor is going to be difficult and challenging. Exercises increase endorphin levels too thereby increasing your happiness quotient, which, in turn, could help you manage hunger pangs better.

Drink coffee guilt-free – If you have adopted the 'skipping breakfast' method, then don't forget to get your cup of coffee (sugar-free, of course) before you set out for the day. Drink more cups of tea and coffee right through the fasting period. Caffeine not only takes the edge off your hunger pangs but also boosts lipolysis thereby increasing fat-burning. Remember no sugar, no cream! One word of caution here; avoid drinking so much coffee that you get addicted to it.

Get sufficient sleep – Sufficient sleep is not just a great friend for everyone but also helps in managing your fasting period efficiently. For example, in the 16:8 method, if your fasting period starts at 8 p.m. after a satiating dinner, and your bedtime is 10 p.m., then a significant part of your fasting period is covered in your sleep. You cannot feel hungry when you are asleep!

Additionally, if for some reason you know you are going to be sleep-deprived; perhaps, working on an important project that is due the next day or any other reason, do not indulge in fasting that day. The stress of the lack of sleep will not make the fasting period more stressful than needed.

Take baby steps – Don't take in the plunge straight into the 18:6 or 20:4 method of intermittent fasting. You will fail even before completing an hour of the fasting period. To an untrained mind, the mere thought of fasting for such a long time can result in undue stress. Therefore, start slow.

Initially, skip breakfast for about 2-3 days a week. Increase the number of such days slowly until you are able to skip breakfast on all 7 days of the week. Then, gradually increase the duration of your fasting period by an hour, and keep increasing until you reach your ideal intermittent fasting method.

First, try only for a couple of days – Give yourself a short test period of not more than 2-3 days. Make it a success for this test period, and you will see that you are hooked for life. It is one of the easiest and most efficient ways of gaining health and losing weight.

Treat IF as a form of learning and not some kind of hurdle to cross – If you treat IF as a hurdle, then the stress of winning and losing will enhance the stress of a new lifestyle. Therefore, don't treat it as a hurdle or a test. Simply look at it as a learning experience the outcome of which is only to learn; there is no win or loss.

For example, don't say this, "I will try intermittent fasting for a couple of days, and if it doesn't work then, I will know I have failed." Instead, tell yourself, "I will try intermittent fasting for a couple of days, see how I feel about it, make notes about my experiences, and take it forward from there."

So, get the right mindset to start off on your journey of intermittent fasting, and work hard to be able to leverage its multiple benefits.

What to Expect in the Initial Days and How to Manage the Issues?

It would be naïve to think that intermittent fasting is going to work like a breeze from Day 1. Your body is suddenly undergoing new and unexpected experiences, and it is thrown off-guard for a while. During this time, your body is going to send you signals of discomfort. You must identify these signals and be able to discern as genuine or only initial problems that will pass with time as your body gets accustomed to the new eating pattern. Here are some classic mental and physical reactions that you could encounter along with some tips on how to manage them:

Hunger Pangs

This is, perhaps, the first and the most prominent experience that you will feel during the initial days of your intermittent fasting journey. The ghrelin hormone is responsible for the hunger pangs. Until now, your body is accustomed to getting food every 3-4 hours. Ghrelin levels peak before mealtimes, and when you eat, the level of ghrelin is reduced.

Now that your body will not get the food, ghrelin levels will continue to peak and drive you into deep levels of hunger pangs with each passing minute. It takes a lot of willpower to counter the effects of hunger. However, your body needs only a couple of days to get used to reduced intake of food and the consequent effect of ghrelin to wear off. Here are some tips to manage hunger pangs:

Include a lot of fiber-rich foods in your meal – Fiber-rich foods are known to reduce appetite. Therefore, ensure your meals have a lot of fiber in the form of raw fruit and vegetables, whole grains, beans and legumes, etc. Fiber-rich foods also have a higher water content helping you to remain full for a long time.

Include soups in your meals – Not only do soups make you feel full resulting in less eating during the rest of the meal but they also give you the required amount of micronutrients from the underlying vegetables and/or meat. Of course, it is important to avoid cream-based and high-fat soups. Consume low-calorie and high-fiber soups such as minestrone or bean soups.

Include salads in your meals – Studies have shown that people who eat low-calorie raw salads before a meal eat less during the meal. A simple crunchy salad of celery, carrots, lettuce, tomatoes, and cucumbers with a dash of salt and pepper is yum, filling, and adds very little calories. The fiber in the vegetables enhances your feeling of fullness too.

Your meals must have foods with all three macronutrients included – Don't leave out any of the macronutrients including carbs, proteins, and fats. Your body will crave for a nutrient that is in less supply leaving you feeling hungry sooner than you would like. Just ensure that every macronutrient is in moderate quantities.

Include a portion of grapefruit and/or oranges in your meals or salads – Research studies have shown that grapefruit and oranges have the highest amount of fiber in the fruit and vegetable family, and help to maintain satiety for a sustained period of time helping you manage your hunger pangs effectively.

Drink plenty of water – Staying hydrated helps you manage hunger pangs. In fact, during the initial days of IF when you are acutely aware of hunger pangs, and you consciously make efforts not to eat and instead choose to drink water, you will notice that often hunger is just a reflection of thirst of boredom.

Be active – Just because you are fasting, you must not reduce your normal activity. You could cut down on high-intensity workout sessions during fasting days. However, continue doing your normal work. The trick with intermittent fasting (until your body gets used to the new eating pattern) is that you must keep your mind occupied and away from thoughts of food. Being active is an effective way to stay focused on things other than food.

Drink calorie-free coffee and tea – Caffeine is an excellent appetite crusher. So include a lot of coffee and tea during your fasting period. Remember to keep it sugar-free and cream-free. A bit of low-fat milk is fine.

And finally, remember feeling hungry is just a natural reminder by your body that it is time for the next meal. Hunger pangs do not translate to muscle loss, death, or anything drastic. Teach your mind to calm down, and choose one or more of the above practical solutions to manage this temporary discomfort.

Cravings

Have you ever told yourself that you will never eat an apple ever again only to reach out for a slice of it in about half an hour? That is how the human mind works. The minute you tell yourself that you will not do something, your mind is so focused on that thing, that you will be compelled to do exactly that thing you didn't want to. Be wary of this feeling when it comes to intermittent fasting.

IF calls for staying away from food, and your mind is invariably going to wander towards food. Specifically, you'll find yourself craving for sweets and refined and processed foods because your mind can easily recall the amazing taste of these foods, and your body wants that glucose hit. Here are some tips to manage cravings:

Drink water – Whenever the craving hits you, drink a glass of water because quite often, cravings are nothing but a reflection of thirst.

Include extra protein in your meals – Proteins reduce cravings and make you full and satiated for a long period of time.

Distract yourself from the craving – Go for a brisk walk or take a shower or do something that you like which will take your mind off the craving. You can also try chewing sugar-free gum.

Plan your meals in advance – When you plan your meals, you avoid spontaneity and the associated concerns regarding what you will eat for your meal. This will reduce temptations and cravings because you will have taken care to include an item you like in your next meal, and that thought will help you manage the desire.

Headaches

Headaches are another common symptom experienced during the early days of intermittent fasting. The causes of these temporary headaches could be lowered blood-sugar levels and stress hormones that are common physiological symptoms of intermittent fasting. With practice, your body will get used to this new routine, and headaches will disappear sooner than later.

Again, keeping yourself hydrated is a good way of preventing headaches while fasting. Ensure you are drinking sufficient amounts of calorie-free liquids in your fasting and feeding windows. Here are some more ways you can manage your stress without medication:

Get yourself a cup of coffee – Caffeine is a great stress-buster and can potentially reduce your headache.

Avoid chewing gum – Chewing gum hurts your jaw and your head. When you have a headache, don't chew gum.

Dim the lights – Whether it is the overhead light or the light from your electronic devices including computers, mobiles, etc. Dim the lights to reduce stress on your eyes.

Practice relaxation techniques – Meditate or do some yoga postures when you have a headache. Chances of pain reduction are very high with these kinds of relaxation techniques.

Low Energy Levels

Mind you, low energy levels are experienced only in the beginning stages. Once your body gets used to fat-burning, you will get an increased boost of energy right through the day. After all, one gram of glucose gives you only 4 calories and one gram of fat gives you 9 calories!

However, before your body becomes an efficient fat-burning machine, the lack of glucose due to fasting will result in lowered energy levels. Here are some tips to manage these initial few days:

- Avoid excessive physical activity including high-intensity training and workouts

- Keep your days as relaxed as possible

- Get some extra sleep

At this juncture, it makes sense to give one more pertinent tip about IF. Don't start your intermittent fasting journey when you are in the middle of an important project at home or at your workplace. The IF routine is going to take some time to get habituated in your head, and therefore, needs the full attention of your body and mind in the initial days. Starting IF in the middle of something important will result in diluted results driving you to wrong conclusions such that IF is not for you.

Irritability

Anger due to hunger is a real phenomenon, and if you have a serious problem with it, then avoiding the IF way is best. However, if you can manage hangry (angry because you are hungry) situations until your body gets accustomed to the new routine, then go ahead, and expect this temporary side-effect to impact your life, and challenge it head-on. Here are some tips:

- Avoid situations that enhance stress during this time including people who are habitual annoyers.

- Focus on activities that make you happy and joyful so that you feel less irritable

- Expect it, and steel your body and mind to be patient for a while

Constipation, Heartburn, and Bloating

Your body is used to releasing digestive enzymes, acids, and hormones during mealtimes. Now, even when the supply of food is not there, these digestive enzymes continue to be released resulting in bloating, heartburn and constipation. These temporary discomforts will continue for a little while until your body gets used to the new eating pattern. The discomfort could range from mild to continuous painful burping. Here are some tips to manage these uncomfortable situations:

- Avoid eating greasy and spicy foods during your feeding time
- Drink plenty of water
- Include a lot of fiber-rich foods to avoid constipation
- Prop yourself up when you sleep

If these discomforts don't disappear, then contact your physician.

Feeling Cold

Feeling cold is a good sign of intermittent fasting. The reason for this cold feeling is that when you fast, there is increased blood flow to fat reserves in your body. The increased blood flow facilitates the movement of fat to muscles where it can be processed for energy release. Also, reduced blood sugar levels also result in a feeling of coldness. Here are some tips to manage this feeling of cold:

- Sip hot tea
- Take warm showers
- Wear extra layers of clothing
- Don't go out into the cold for long

Overeating

Yes, this is a definite side-effect, especially during the first few days. The reason for overeating during the feeding window could be many including:

- A misconceived notion that it is alright to eat whatever you want and how much ever you want during the feeding time

- Happiness at completing the fasting without eating a morsel of food can result in forgetting to keep control of food consumption when the fasting period is over

- Overexcitement about eating during the feeding time

- A sense of dread that hunger pangs will hit you again during the next fasting period, and therefore, it is best to stuff yourself with extra food

Overeating during the feeding time results in weight gain making you think that IF is ineffective. It is important to keep your portions and food consumption normal during feeding time. You must eat as if you are not fasting. Only then will IF work the way it is explained in this book.

Be mindful of your first meal after the fasting period. Plan your meals in advance. In fact, prepare them, and put them into boxes so that you can simply take out the food and eat. There is no need to think much, which can be quite a strain after the fasting period. The strain of thinking of what to eat after the fasting period is bound to make you simply reach out to a couple of slices of pizza and/or a plate of fries with hamburger! Therefore, planning and prepping your feeding time meals in advance is the best way to avoid overeating.

Increased Trips to the Bathroom

You will be drinking large quantities of water to keep yourself hydrated right through the day including your fasting and feeding times. This situation is naturally going to increase your trips to the bathroom. However, there is no way around this except to make the trip whenever nature calls. Do not reduce the intake of water to reduce your bathroom trips.

And finally, always listen to your body and follow its needs. The side-effects mentioned above typically last for a period of 1 to 3 weeks. If any of these side-effects beyond this time or you feel unusually comfortable, stop intermittent fasting.

How to Ease Yourself into Intermittent Fasting

Many of the side-effects of IF cannot be really avoided. They can only be managed. The most effective way of getting into your IF journey is to slowly ease yourself into it. Instead of going from 6 meals a day to 2 meals a day on your first attempt, you must take baby steps, and gradually increase the intensity and duration of the fasting period. Here are some tips to help you with that:

Day 1 – *Nothing after dinner*

On the first day, do not eat after dinner. Eat all your meals right through the day, but do not eat anything after your dinner. It is quite unlikely that you are hungry after your dinner at 7. However, it is not uncommon for you to snack on popcorn or chips or a cup of ice-cream after dinner as you relax in front of the TV alone or with your family. Avoid this on Day 1. If you are used to this, then getting through the night on Day 1 without that snack might be challenging. Here are some helpful tips:

- Replace popcorn/chips/ice-cream with warm herbal tea or plain water.

- Brush your teeth immediately after your dinner. Not only does the minty taste of toothpaste help in curbing cravings, but your subconscious mind also gets a signal that you are done eating for the day which, in turn, helps turn off the activity of ghrelin hormone.

- Go straight to bed.

Day 2 – *Delayed breakfast*

Even if you are an early bird and wake up at 6 a.m., you will have finished 11 hours of fasting. If you wake up at around 7 a.m., which is typical for most people, then you will be 12 hours into your fasting period. So, persist a little more and delay your breakfast.

Anyway, you may be in a rush to get ready for the office, and busy with all your other activities. So, have a cup of coffee, pack a light breakfast (maybe sandwiches made with whole grain bread), and eat it along with your morning coffee in the office at 10 a.m. that's it. You will have already completed about 14 hours of fasting time. Here's what your day will look like:

- 10 a.m. – breakfast

- 12 noon – it may be lunchtime, but it is quite likely that you are not hungry because of the delayed breakfast; so, feel free to push your lunchtime to 2 p.m.

- 2 p.m. – lunch

- 5 p.m. – a little snack

- 7 p. m. – dinner, and nothing more; just like Day 1

Day 3 – *Avoid the evening snack*

Continue the same food timetable as Day 1 and Day 2 except remove the evening snack. Here are some tips to help you overcome the snack craving:

- Remind yourself that your dinner is only a couple of hours away, and you are really not very hungry right now. It is only a habit that is being triggered.

- Have a cup of sugar-free coffee, tea, or lemonade.

- Stay active and indulge in some activity until dinnertime so that you don't focus on your craving, which is temporary and will go away if you don't respond to it.

Day 4 – *Delay breakfast by another hour*

So, instead of breakfast at 10 a.m. have your breakfast at 11 a.m. Then, you will be able to delay your lunch to 3 p.m., and your dinner at 7 p.m. that's it. You have managed to achieve the 16:8 method of intermittent fasting within four days of slowly easing your body and mind into the process.

Nearly all the therapeutic effects of intermittent fasting will kick in with this 16:8 method also referred to as the Leangains method. When you are thoroughly fixed into this regimen with absolutely no sign of any side-effects whatsoever, try and extend your intermittent fasting to the more rigorous ones.

For example, moving into the 18:6 method can happen seamlessly after a fortnight of strictly following the 16:8 regimen. Keep to the 18:6 regimen for as long as your body takes to get accustomed to it. When you are fine with it, then you can move on to the 20-hour, the 24-hour, and the alternate day methods, which are more difficult to manage. However, if you are patient with yourself, and take baby steps at each stage, you will notice that not only are you losing weight but also becoming far more energetic than before your IF days.

Chapter Five: Intermittent Fasting and Weight Loss

Weight Loss is one of the most or even the most significant benefits of intermittent fasting. Therefore, it makes sense to dedicate an entire chapter to this crucial element of IF. Before we go into how IF benefits weight loss, you need to correctly understand some of the misconceived aspects of our metabolism.

Important Points to Remember About Our Metabolism

The following points about your metabolism will help you understand how intermittent fasting is most effective for weight loss:

Metabolism takes place in every cell of your body – It is common to hear people talking about human metabolism like it is an organ or a body part, which you can control. In truth, metabolism is nothing but a series of chemical reactions that take place in each cell. The basic metabolic rate (BMR) is the minimum amount of energy (measured in calories) needed for your body functions to take place smoothly when you are at complete rest. It is the total energy needed to keep the different cells, tissues, organs, and organ systems to function normally and without a hitch when you are at rest.

A significant portion (nearly 50%) of your body's basic metabolic rate is used by for the functioning of the major organs including the heart, brain, kidneys and liver. The rest of the BMR is used by the digestive system, the body's muscles, fats, and others.

BMR accounts for the largest amount of calories burned by your body – Your body burns calories in three different ways including:

- BMR or the energy needed to continue your body's normal functioning when you are at rest

- Thermic effect is the energy required to break down consumed food into energy

- The energy needed for the physical activity you do

Studies have revealed that BMR accounts for nearly 60-80% of the energy burned during the day. Breaking down food takes up about 10%. Energy for physical activity uses up only 10-30% although people in high-performance sports could use up a little more.

This observation is especially useful for people who think that if they exercise enough, they can eat what they want and when they want. The truth is that weight loss, of course, requires a combination of reduced intake and increased usage of calories.

Metabolism varies between different people, and there is no scientific explanation for the phenomenon – Two people with similar body weight, size, and composition can have different metabolism, and currently, there is no scientific explanation for this difference. Though some studies seem to connect metabolism to lean mass, fat tissue, age, gender, and perhaps, genetics, there is no conclusive evidence as yet for the anomaly.

Advancing age slows down metabolism – It has been proven that advancing age definitely slows down metabolism. Even if your muscle and fat composition at 60 is the same as it was when you were 20, the BMR will show a decreased figure now. The decline of metabolism is believed to start as early as 18 years.

Slowing metabolism does not prevent you from losing weight and keeping the lost weight off – Multiple experiments have revealed that it is highly possible to lose weight and keep it off even when your metabolism is reducing. The trick is to identify and make positive lifestyle changes that you can adhere to over a sustained period of time, preferably your entire lifetime. Intermittent fasting is definitely one such lifestyle change that is sustainable and positively impacts your long-term weight-loss program without creating undue stress and anxiety that are normally associated with crash diets.

Intermittent Fasting and Weight Loss

You already read about how the body has two sources of energy; one from the consumed food in the form of glucose (fed state), and the other from stored food primarily in the form of fat and some of it in the form of glycogen (fasted state). The crucial point to remember is that your body can access energy from only one of these two sources at a time.

For example, if it is in the fed state, then your body accesses only the energy from the consumed food. And when it is in the fasted state, it can access only the energy from stored fat. The body cannot access energy both from consumed food and stored food simultaneously.

When the body is in the fed state, it is easy to use the glucose coming from the consumed for energy, and that is the default option. During the fed state, insulin levels are high which triggers the fat-burning process or lipolysis and the conversion of stored glycogen to glucose (gluconeogenesis) to shut down.

Typically, when you have not yet started the fasting regimen, and you consume 3-4 meals a day, this is what is happening right through the day; the fat-burning process is completely shut down. Now, in the same situation, let us see what happens when we sleep during which time you don't eat any food. No consumption of food translates to lowered insulin levels, which, in turn, signals the body to start using energy from its stored reserves. That is the reason you wake up instead of dying at night even though you have not eaten for nearly 10-12 hours.

When you voluntary fast during the day, the same thing happens. The insulin level falls, which is the trigger for the body to switch to, stored food for its energy needs. So, first, the body reaches out to the limited supply of stored glycogen in the liver and muscles, and when this is exhausted, it turns to the abundant supply of fat energy from the adipose tissues deposited all over the body.

Suppose your BMR is 2000 calories. This means you need 2000 calories of energy to simply get the basic physiological functions in your body to take place seamlessly. When you fast for 24 hours, this requirement of

2000 calories is taken from the large reserve of fat energy stored in your body. By the way, 2000 calories accounts for about half a pound of fat!

This process of reaching out to stored food for energy is the reason for human survival across millennia. If we didn't have this natural mechanism, we would have been wiped out millions of years ago because food was not always available in plenty to our hunter-gatherer ancestors, and therefore, intermittent fasting is a natural and healthy process for weight loss.

The summary is this: the body either uses fat or stores fat. When food is available in plenty, then it stores fat, and when food is scarce, the body uses fat. The critical regulator of this process is insulin, and therefore, it makes sense to spend some time on this crucial digestive hormone.

The Significance of Insulin in Intermittent Fasting

The differences in the levels of insulin are what triggers the body to switch between consumed food and stored food for its energy. When insulin levels are high, your body uses consumed food for its energy, and when the insulin levels are low, it uses the stored food for energy.

So, when you use traditional ways of diets to lose fat, you are most often compelled to eat about 4-6 times a day resulting in your insulin levels remaining high at all times. This situation ensures your body hardly ever reaches out to the stored food for its energy needs. As insulin is high, your body's energy needs have to come from consumed food as it cannot access stored food during this time.

So, in conventional diets, suppose you restrict your calorie intake from 2000 to 1500 a day. You do this in the hope that you lose weight because your body is consuming less energy than the BMR. However, as you are eating 4-6 times a day insulin levels are always at high levels right through the day. Initially, you do lose weight from these diets.

However, as your body can never access the stored food or fat reserves, it makes adjustments to reduce the BMR itself to 1500 calories resulting in reduced metabolism. Therefore, after the initial few days (when you do lose weight), with conventional diets, the weight loss plateaus because your metabolism has slowed down to adjust to the new calorie intake.

Not only does your weight loss stop, but reduced metabolism makes you feel exhausted and irritable. And soon, your body weight increases which makes you want to give up the endeavor. So, you increase your calorie intake to 1700 per day, which is still less than 2000 (your initial BMR). However, now you are in a situation wherein your BMR is 1500, and you are consuming 1700 calories resulting in weight gain slowly but surely.

Therefore, the crucial element is weight loss is not only reducing calories but also reducing insulin levels. Insulin is the switch fat storage and fat usage. You want your body to remain primarily in the fat usage stage, and to achieve this, you must reduce insulin levels. The most natural way to reduce insulin levels is to put your body increasingly in a fasted state. That is why, intermittent fasting is the most natural and effective means of fat loss, and consequently, weight loss.

Critical Points to Remember for Effective Weight Loss

Weight loss is primarily caused by fat loss, which happens if we eat fewer calories than we need each day; a phenomenon referred to as 'calorie deficit.' To achieve this calorie deficit, intermittent fasting has to work in conjunction with the following elements:

Quality of food – Avoid unprocessed refined foods completely, and stick to wholesome, wholegrain, and nutritious foods.

Calorie consumption – Making up for the loss of calorie intake during fasting by overeating in the feeding window will not help you lose weight in any way. In fact, you will end up gaining weight even after attempting IF for a sufficiently long time.

Patience – Your body needs time to get used to a new way of living. If you rush through the initial days without giving your body sufficient leeway to get accustomed to the various changes brought on by IF, it is going to get confused which can have disastrous results.

Consistency – IF has to be implemented consistently for effective benefits to be achieved. You cannot expect to do IF for a couple of months and revert back to your old eating pattern. It is a lifestyle change that has to be put in place so that it lasts consistently throughout your life.

Exercise – Fasting does not allow you to lead a sedentary lifestyle. You have to continue to do whatever you did before you started your fasting regimen. Combining exercise and fasting is believed to multiply the fat loss process resulting in more effective fat loss than if the two elements were tried separately.

FAQs on Weight Loss by Intermittent Fasting

Here are some FAQs on how intermittent fasting affects weight loss. Most of your questions will be found here.

How much of weight loss can I expect with intermittent fasting?

Weight loss by intermittent fasting depends on multiple factors including:

- The extent of your fasting window
- The fasting method you choose
- What you consume during the feeding period

However, when you reach a fasting duration of 16-20 hours a day on a consistent basis, then you can potentially lose 2-3 pounds of fat each week. In addition to losing weight, the other 'cool' benefit of intermittent fasting is how it simplifies the meal planning and prep work because you have now reduced your meals from 4-6 a day to 1-3 a day!

Can I continue to exercise when I fast?

Yes, absolutely. You might have to reduce your high-intensity workouts during the initial days when your energy levels are slightly low. This is a short period of time when your body is still learning to burn fat efficiently and your food consumption is also reduced which results in reduced energy levels. During this phase, which usually lasts for a couple of weeks, it might be a good idea not to indulge in high-intensity workouts to conserve energy.

In fact, once your body gets accustomed to burning fat, your energy levels will see an increase, and you will find it easy to remain physically and mentally alert right through the day without signs of fatigue or hunger driving you crazy even on highly active days.

Is Fasting Safe?

Fasting is one of the most natural methods to burn stored fat in the human body and has been in existence since time immemorial. You are not force-feeding your body with anything at all. There are no new elements or ingredients that are being tried in this method. You are only driving your body to access its own stored food, and therefore, intermittent fasting is one of the safest and most natural methods of weight loss.

However, there are certain contraindications such as pregnancy, an underlying medical condition such as diabetes, and more for which you must take care. These aspects have been discussed in detail in Chapter Two.

Chapter Six: Mistakes to Avoid and Other Important Information about Intermittent Fasting

Now that you know a lot of information including various benefits of intermittent fasting, it is time to learn about some of the most common avoidable mistakes that beginners do. This knowledge will help you plan your IF journey well and ensure you achieve success. Here are some easily discernible and avoidable mistakes of novices:

Choosing the Wrong Method of Intermittent Fasting

Chapter Three discusses the different methods of intermittent fasting, and nearly all of them are effective to leverage multiple benefits of IF. It is imperative that you choose a method that is aligned with your personal needs and lifestyle. Do not get carried away by what others are doing. Think objectively and make the right choice.

For example, the 5:2 method calls for reducing your calorie intake to just about 500-600 calories on the fasting days. Now, if you lead an active life with a family and kids, full-time work that is quite stressful, and regular visits to the gym, then this method might not be the best because you will not be able to maintain your active lifestyle on the fasting days with significantly reduced calorie intake.

With this kind of lifestyle, maybe starting off with the simple 12-hour fasting, and gradually increasing it to the 16:8 or the 18:6 method might be the best option. However, you must make this choice on your own. For beginners especially, it is important to start small to prevent feeling disillusioned with failures driven by setting unreasonable expectations.

Moving Excessively Fast in the Intermittent Fasting Journey

If, for example, you are used to 5 meals a day, and you choose to move to the 16:8 or even trying to fast for 10 hours at a stretch during daytime might be counterproductive to success. Your body needs time to adjust itself to the new eating pattern. Start with baby steps, and ensure you don't rush through the journey to reach your peak level of intermittent fasting quickly.

The results of impatience will be disastrous, and you are bound to feel disappointed and dissatisfied. Use the pattern mentioned in Chapter Four to ease yourself into intermittent fasting slowly but surely. This approach will result in sustained success.

The same logic holds good for your exercise regimen during IF. If, for example, you are used to morning workouts, and now, you are starting off your IF regimen by skipping breakfast, you might have to change your workout timings to a more suitable time, at least until your body is set in the new ways.

So, the crucial aspect to remember is to be patient with yourself and your body. It takes time to make changes, especially sustainable positive ones. Don't be overambitious and spoil your chances of success.

Obsessed with Keeping Perfect Time

For example, if your lunch is to be at 12 noon, you don't have to wait for the stroke of twelve to eat. Don't obsess over time. Eat when you are sufficiently close to the end of the fasting period. A few minutes this side or that side is not really going to make a difference to your results.

The problem with this kind of obsession is that it creates undue stress making it easier to give up your efforts. Therefore, don't waste your resources obsessing over micromanaging your intermittent fasting timetable. Just relax and listen to your body and mind.

Giving Up Trying Very Soon

Setting your body into the right rhythm of intermittent fasting takes a lot of effort and a lot of time. The initial few days are the toughest because your body and mind are battling with multiple new mindset and physiological changes. It is natural for your body to resist changes of any kind, and it will create discomforts in various forms (discussed in detail in Chapter Four) to try and dissuade you from the effort.

Acknowledge this natural response of your body, learn about the different ways it will resist, and prepare yourself mentally and physically to manage them. With patience and persistence, you will notice your energy levels slowly rising, your ability to manage hunger pangs increasing, and your body slowly adapting to fat-burning techniques. Until this happens, don't give up on yourself. Success lies on the other side of hard work.

Excessive Eating During Feeding Periods

Until you recognize the correct balance between eating and overeating, you must err on the side of caution, and eat less than you planned. This approach is important to ensure you don't overeat during your feeding window.

Initially, you will feel so famished after a fasting period that you could easily end up eating more than you need defeating the very purpose of fasting to reduce calorie intake. Be wary of this mistake, and eat your meals mindfully to prevent overeating. Use the tips and tricks given in Chapter Four on how to prevent overeating.

Eating Very Little During Feeding Periods

As you get deeper into your fasting regimen, you will need increasingly smaller quantities of food to fill satiated. You don't feel very hungry after some time into, and many times, it is possible that you forget that your fasting period is over, and you need to eat!

It is important not to under-eat as well because the lack of sufficient nutrients could potentially lead to other health issues. Additionally, your focus and your attention span could be affected preventing you from reaching your peak performance levels. Therefore, ensure you never dip below the 1200 calorie mark on an average every week.

Eating the Wrong Kinds of Foods

Intermittent fasting is not as strict as other diets when it comes to eating what you want. However, it is not a free-for-all niche too. You cannot eat pizzas, fries, and burgers for every meal. It is critical that you nourish your body with all three macronutrients in well-balanced meals.

This balanced approach will not only keep you satiated for a sustained period of time but also allow your body to be nourished in a healthy way. Your brain, your muscle, and all other organs will develop healthily when macronutrients are available in sufficient quantities.

Not Being Active

Fasting can make you very restless because your mind is already quite stressed out about going hungry. If you cannot find ways to distract your mind and body, breaking the fast (even when you are not hungry) will be the first and only thing that captures your attention. Therefore, don't stop your normal activities when you start off your IF journey. Live as you normally do. Only follow the eating pattern as described in this book.

Overusing Caffeine

When you skip breakfast, drinking one or two cups of coffee is the most natural response to stave off hunger. However, overuse of caffeine can be disastrous because if you don't stop yourself with a couple of cups, you are going to get addicted to caffeine, and with any addiction, the purpose of the original intermittent fasting journey will be forgotten.

Best Foods for Intermittent Fasting

Water – Whether you are in the fasting or feasting window, the importance of being can never be overstated. Water is the most important element in each and every cell of the body. It is imperative that no cell of your body dies due to the lack of water. Hydration helps to overcome negative side-effects such as headaches, hunger pangs, and more.

The amount of water needed varies for each individual. The sign of your body being well-hydrated is that your urine should be a pale yellow color. Dark yellow urine reveals your body is not hydrated enough. Dehydration causes headaches, lightheadedness, and fatigue.

If you combine lack of water with fasting, then disaster is sure to strike. So, avoid this situation by drinking plenty of water. If you find water plain and boring, add a dash of lime, soak some slices of cucumber, and add a couple of sprigs of mint to boost the taste and texture of water. You will love this.

Fish – Fish is a rich source of proteins and healthy fats. Fish is also very rich in Vitamin D that is crucial for calcium absorption. Moreover, if you are limited food intake, then fish referred to as 'brain food' can be an excellent supplement for improved functioning of the brain. Make sure you include fish in your meals.

Avocado – The high concentration of healthy monosaturated fats in avocado ensures you remain satiated for a sustained period of time. Multiple studies have revealed that eating even half an avocado can stave off hunger pangs for long hours.

Cruciferous vegetables – The cruciferous vegetable family consists of cauliflower, cabbage, broccoli, and Brussel sprouts. These veggies are full of fiber; an unmissable element for the success of intermittent fasting. Moreover, these veggies help to keep constipation and other digestive tract-related disorders at bay. Fiber-rich foods also keep you satiated for a long time preventing the onset of painful hunger pangs.

Beans and legumes – Black beans, chickpeas, lentils, and peas are excellent sources of low-carb proteins allowing you to get both these macronutrients in balanced quantities. In fact, these listed beans and legumes are known to decrease body weight even without reducing calorie intake.

Potatoes – We are not talking potato fries that come with hamburgers or chips that come with fish chips. We are talking about well-cooked potatoes because the carbs in this vegetable are known to be one of the most satiating carbs in the world. Baked potatoes with skin on, and other such healthy and oil-free potatoes dishes are great additions to your meals.

Probiotics – Your gut's flora and fauna are responsible for a healthy digestive process. When your stomach is empty, then these gut flora and fauna can create unpleasant side-effects such as constipation. Probiotic-rich foods such as sauerkraut, kombucha, and kefir are excellent to counter these negative effects.

Eggs – Eggs are complete meals by themselves, and are so easy to cook. The protein-rich food is excellent to keep your hunger-free for a long period of time. Studies have shown that people who ate an egg in the morning felt far less hungry than people who did not consume eggs.

Berries – Strawberries, blueberries, and other members of the berry family are rich in Vitamin C; an essential micronutrient for the health of your immune system. Additionally, some studies have revealed that eating flavonoid-rich berries in the long term can reduce your BMI.

Nuts – While nuts have a big calorific value as compared to raw fruit and vegetables, they contain polyunsaturated fat, which is considered 'good fat.' A few nuts to snack on will take care of your fat needs for the day. In fact, walnuts are believed to change certain physiological markers that affect appetite and satiety.

Whole grains – Whole grains might be all carbs on the face of it. However, they are rich in proteins as well as fibers and keep you feeling full and hunger-free for a sustained period of time. Studies have also revealed that eating whole grains instead of refined foods can potentially increase your metabolism. Therefore, make sure you include bulgur wheat, amaranth, kamut, sorghum, millets, and other such cereals in some of your meals.

Foods to Avoid During Intermittent Fasting

Sugar – You must avoid sugars of all kinds including honey, artificial sweeteners, etc. Drinking sweetened tea or coffee is like eating a fistful of candies resulting in the spiking of insulin levels almost immediately. When insulin is released, the effectiveness of your intermittent fasting is lost. Studies have revealed that even commercially available zero-calorie artificial sweeteners trigger the release of insulin. Therefore, it is best to completely avoid sugars during intermittent fasting.

Foods with hidden calories – Multiple foods in the market call themselves sugar-free but sneak in some calories in a couple of ingredients. For example, clear broth, bottled water, etc. could have ingredients with calorific values that could negatively impact the effectiveness of intermittent fasting. Be cautious about these items, and read the label, and ensure it is truly zero-calorie product before consuming.

Refined foods – All kinds of processed and refined foods are to be avoided because they trigger the highest levels of insulin release.

Conclusion

Intermittent fasting is not some kind of new diet that has been introduced to the world in the recent past. It is as old as humankind. Starting from our hunter-gatherer ancestors who fasted from compulsion and food shortage to the wise men in nearly all ancient civilizations to religions, fasting was a way of healing, resting the body, and an act of self-control and penitence.

Modern science is only ratifying what our ancestors already knew and implemented without a doubt. Intermittent fasting is, therefore, nothing but a new name given to an age-old custom that got lost somewhere in the depths of development, wealth, and progress. It makes sense to complete this book by summarizing the amazing benefits of intermittent fasting so that you feel motivated to implement in your life.

Shifts our metabolism from glucose to fat – Our metabolic fire has to burn continuously as long as we are alive. The fuel for this fire comes either from consumed food or stored food. The unfortunate aspect of modern life is that many of us have stored food in excess of our needs. Intermittent fasting triggers the body to reach out to the stored food for its fuel so that it is used up and we are left with the right balance of stored food and consumed food in our systems. Effectively, IF triggers fat metabolism resulting in all the benefits listed below.

Reduces fat content all over the body including stubborn belly fat – When the body goes into fat metabolism, it uses fat sources from all over the body including from the belly area which consists of stubborn fat (referred to as visceral fat) that is the most difficult to burn. So, you can easily get a flat stomach if you persist in your IF efforts.

Increases energy levels – Fat metabolism results in more energy being released than carb metabolism. Therefore, after the initial few days during which time your body is learning to become an efficient fat-burning machine, you will feel more energetic than before with improved productivity.

Reduced inflammation and oxidative stress – Intermittent fasting results in reduced inflammation and oxidative stress which, in turn, benefits your body in many ways including:

- Slows down aging

- Fights against multiple health disorders caused by inflammation and oxidative stress

- Improves skin texture and smoothness

Frees up energy for more productive work – Intermittent fasting is the most natural way of resting your digestive system that needs to work almost without a break. The body's focus is shifted from digesting food to other important work such as cell repair and maintenance, clearing of toxic wastes from the body, and more.

Intermittent fasting is not some kind of crash diet. It is a life-changing habit that is expected to last a lifetime and brings with it a host of benefits that has immensely positive impact on your life. It would be naïve not to try this method of losing weight and leading a healthier life than before. You would be doing a disservice to yourself if you didn't try intermittent fasting and leverage its multiple benefits simply because of fears and biases. So, go ahead, reread the book, make sure you have understood how IF works, and plunge right in.

www.ingramcontent.com/pod-product-compliance
Lightning Source LLC
LaVergne TN
LVHW021304080526
838199LV00090B/6013